A Short Introduction to Abraham Kuyper's Lectures on Calvinism

A Short Introduction to Abraham Kuyper's Lectures on Calvinism

JESSE M. SUMPTER

For Kate, a loyal friend and spouse
who joins me in
the "high calling to push the development of this world
to an even higher stage,
for the sake of God."

Francis Drake Press
Moscow, Idaho

Jesse M. Sumpter, *A Short Introduction to Abraham Kuyper's Lectures on Calvinism*,

Copyright © 2020 by Jesse M. Sumpter. All Rights Reserved. No part of this publication may be reproduced, stored in a retrieval system, or transmitted in any form or by any means, electronic, mechanical, photocopying, recording, scanning, or otherwise, except as permitted under Section 107 or 108 of the 1967 United States Copyright Act, without either the prior written permission of the author, or authorization through payment of the appropriate per-copy fee to the Copyright Clearance Center, Inc., 222 Rosewood Drive, Danvers, MA 01023, (978) 750-8400, or on the web at www.copyright.com. Requests to the author for permission should be addressed to jesse.sumpter@gmail.com.

Cover design and interior layout: Valerie Anne Bost
Cover texture image: unsplash.com/@scottwebb

Version: 20201114print

Contents

Introduction 1

Calvinism: A Life System.................... 7

Calvinism and Religion 15

Calvinism and Politics 25

Calvinism and Science...................... 35

Calvinism and Art 45

Calvinism and the Future 55

Additional Resources for Further Study 65

Introduction

Kuyper's lectures on Calvinism are some of the best theological discussions from the last century. In these lectures, you get two important theologians at the same time: John Calvin and Abraham Kuyper. Both of these men have shaped history and theology in important ways. This series of lectures illustrates how Calvin's work and teaching impact a variety of topics: politics, science, art, and religion. These lectures are also an excellent introduction to Kuyper's work. Here you will find many of his key ideas: God's sovereignty in the world, God-ordained spheres of authority, and God's election of his people. Kuyper knew his own time well, and he had a great eye for what was to come. Learning from

Kuyper offers us a chance to get a better picture of our world and how we can work to bring the gospel to coming generations.

In this short introduction, I am interested in letting Abraham Kuyper speak for himself. You will find many direct (and sometimes long) quotes from him. After each quote, I've included in parentheses the page numbers in the edition of the lectures that I used. I hope that my added commentary and explanations will bring Kuyper into our time and provide a contemporary voice to dialogue with.

What Kuyper offers in his lectures is a way for Christians to better understand the high calling we have from God to disciple the nations. Our calling is as big as the cosmos. While that might seem like an impossible task for man, it is not so for God. Kuyper points the way forward as we walk by faith, calling all spheres to submit to the lordship of Jesus.

BIOGRAPHY

Abraham Kuyper was born on October 29, 1837, in the Netherlands. He grew up in the Dutch Reformed Church, and his father was a minister in that denomination. Abraham was homeschooled. He went on to study philosophy, theology, and literature at the university level, graduating summa cum laude.

He was a minister in the Dutch Reformed Church, but he saw corruption there and led a reforming movement. This movement encouraged a clearer separation of church and state.

Kuyper was elected to parliament in 1874 and began a successful career in politics. He served as prime minister of the Netherlands from 1901 to 1905.

In his work, he encouraged the antithesis between Christianity and other worldly philosophies, especially modernism and liberal theology. He also promoted Calvinism and helped develop the political philosophy of sphere sovereignty for the church, state, and family.

In 1898, Kuyper was invited by B.B. Warfield to give a series of lectures, sponsored by the L.P. Stone Foundation, at Princeton Theological Seminary. Kuyper gave six lectures on Calvinism as a life system.

KEY IDEAS

Before looking at these specific lectures, it is important to understand three key ideas in Kuyper's work. There are many other important ideas to consider from Kuyper, but I will leave the reader to pursue those on his own.

The first key idea is the lordship of Jesus. One cannot understand Kuyper without this key piece.

The most famous quote from Kuyper that everyone should know is this: "Oh, no single piece of our mental world is to be hermetically sealed off from the rest, and there is not a square inch in the whole domain of our human existence over which Christ, who is sovereign over all, does not cry: 'Mine!'" (1880 Inaugural Lecture, Free University of Amsterdam). Jesus is King right now, and he is ruling over everything. There is nothing that escapes his judging eye and his jurisdiction. This is the key principle that drove Kuyper to do so much in the realms of theology, philosophy, and politics.

The second key idea is proposing Calvinism as a life system. Kuyper saw John Calvin's work as teaching what the Bible taught about the impact of the gospel. The gospel impacts everything. It impacts our relationship with God, our relationship with man, and our relationship with the world. In the first area, the Bible teaches that there is no mediator between each man and God except for the God-Man, Jesus. Kuyper says, "At every moment of our existence, our entire spiritual life rests in God Himself" (Lectures on Calvinism, 21).[1] Based on this, Kuyper

---

1. Kuyper, Abraham, *Lectures on Calvinism*, originally published in 1931, Cosimo, Inc, 2007. All citations come from this version of *Lectures on Calvinism* unless otherwise noted. Likewise, all italics are in the original. Page numbers in parentheses throughout will refer to this edition.

then drives to the second point, that we "have no claim whatsoever to lord over one another, and that we stand as equals before God, and consequently equal as man to man" (27). From this flows the third principle, how we relate to the world. Kuyper sets before us "the recognition that in the whole world the curse is restrained by grace, that the life of the world is to be honored in its independence, and that we must, in every domain, discover the treasures and develop the potencies hidden by God in nature and in human life" (31).

The third key idea from Kuyper springs from these previous ones: spheres of authority. In looking at these spheres, we see that Kuyper was not an egalitarian. He understood that God has established authorities in the world and that God has ordained them to maintain good order. Kuyper taught that there are three key governments: family, church, and state. These three operate on the foundation of self-government, which requires that each man must submit directly to Jesus' lordship. The family is set apart to rule over the needs surrounding reproduction, food, clothing, shelter, and education. The church is set apart to rule over the spiritual needs of teaching and preaching the word of God and administering the sacraments. The state is set apart to defend its people and punish evil. These are established so that each sphere does its own work but also provides accountability to the other two. The state needs to focus on its tasks and not overreach into the others (e.g., administering the sacraments or spanking the children). Nor can the family play the church or vice versa. Each sphere has its own authority and role to fulfill in the world.

With these key ideas in place, one can dig deeper into Kuyper's philosophy and theology. There is much to study and learn here. My hope is that the following chapters will encourage you to begin a longer journey of reading and studying Kuyper's vision and work in greater depth.

Calvinism: A Life System

In his first lecture, Abraham Kuyper sets out his reason for lecturing on Calvinism. He argues that modernism is on the rise and that a solid theological foundation is needed to combat this threat. He proposes Calvinism as this true foundation because it addresses every aspect of man's condition. Kuyper adds that Calvinism is not tied to any one country or people group, so it is a truly catholic force that is able to bring good to the whole world.

NEED FOR A LIFE SYSTEM
First, Kuyper sets out the need of the day. In 1898, Kuyper understood the coming threat of modernism,

and he understood the danger it posed to Christianity. In this first lecture, Kuyper observes, "Two *life systems* are wrestling with one another, in mortal combat" (11). There is no neutral ground between these two life systems. He says that this struggle is happening in Europe and in America. He describes the two sides this way: "Modernism is bound to build a world of its own from the data of the natural man, and to construct man himself from the data of nature; while, on the other hand, all those who reverently bend the knee to Christ and worship Him as the Son of the living God, and God himself, are bent upon saving the 'Christian heritage'" (11). The worldview of naturalism and supernaturalism cannot stand together. One of them must win in the end.

Kuyper suggests that what is needed for the Christian side to win is a truly principled system that can respond to the deep attacks of modernism. He says, "If the battle is to be fought with honor and with a hope of victory, then *principle* must be arrayed against *principle*" (11). It is not enough to have an answer for an atheist or an answer for a Darwinist; the only method of attack that will succeed is one that has a sure foundation that can provide answers integrated across the board. These other systems of belief have something to say about everything; Christians must also have a position that can respond to anything and everything. Kuyper argues that Calvinism provides that system.

Kuyper says, "Calvinism, as the only decisive, lawful, and consistent defence for Protestant nations against encroaching, and overwhelming modernism—this of itself was bound to be my theme" (12). He points to all the great nations in his time: "Calvinism has liberated Switzerland, the Netherlands, and England, and in the Pilgrim Fathers has provided the impulse to the prosperity of the United States" (14–15). Calvinism was the impulse behind true freedom in these nations, and it will be the source of freedom for the rest of the world as well.

CALVINISM IS A LIFE SYSTEM

Kuyper then lays out that Calvinism is a full life system because it deals with man's relation to God, man's relation to man, and man's relation to the world.

In the first area, the Bible teaches that there is no mediator between each man and God except for the God-Man, Jesus. Kuyper says, "At every moment of our existence, our entire spiritual life rests in God Himself" (21). This means there is no human priest or church institution that stands between God and each man. Each and every Christian lives his life *coram deo*, before the presence of God. This means that

God calls each man to a specific job and task in the world. This also means that each man will stand before Jesus as the Judge, and each man will answer for how he has lived his life. It is only in the presence of God that a man can find true freedom in this world.

Kuyper then drives to his second point, that we "have no claim whatsoever to lord over one another, and that we stand as equals before God, and consequently equal as man to man" (27). If every Christian is a priest before God, then there is no one who stands between each man and God. Every Christian man stands directly before Jesus the king. This is the foundation of all earthly freedom. It is also the foundation of the good differences that God has established in the world: male and female, husband and wife, parents and children, teacher and students, king and subjects. Each of these roles is given by God, our heavenly Father, and so we must fulfill our roles in obedience to his divine will.

On the other hand, modernism hates all differences. Kuyper rightly recognized, over a hundred years ago, the end game of modernism: "Finally modernism, which denies and abolishes every difference, cannot rest until it has made woman man and man woman, and, putting every distinction on a common level, kills life by placing it under the ban of uniformity" (27). God has assigned each person to a specific role and task, and it is only in the presence of God that these roles can be understood. This means that only a supernatural life-system can explain the true and real difference between men and women, husbands and wives, parents and children, etc. A life system based on naturalism has no room for a divine calling. This means that naturalism will ultimately collapse everything into a single blob of matter which removes all distinctions and all differences.

Kuyper's third point concerns our relation to the world: "Henceforth the curse should no longer rest upon the *world* itself, but upon that which is *sinful* in it, and instead of monastic flight *from* the world the duty is now emphasized of serving God *in* the world, in every position in life" (30). The Spirit of God calls us to embrace all of life. There is no corner or inch that can escape the reach and authority of Jesus the King. We are not called to hide or ignore the world. We are called to proclaim Jesus to all of it. Kuyper says we must recognize that "in the whole world the curse is restrained by grace, that the life of the world is to be honored in its independence, and that we must, in every domain, discover the treasures and develop the potencies hidden by God in nature and in human life" (31). Kuyper's vision for the Christian life, as one of discovery, is vastly refreshing. We are not just passing through some foreign realm but rather we are here to tend and care and explore. There is much to do. We need Christians who are fathers, mothers, teachers, mathematicians, scientists, doctors, astronauts, politicians, ambassadors, senators, pastors, etc. Kuyper rightly understood that Calvinism, in submitting to the vision of Jesus, offers us a task that is truly global. Given this vast goal, we are merely at the beginning of that mission.

CALVINISM BRINGS FREEDOM TO NATIONS

In the final part of his lecture, Kuyper says that Calvinism presents a truly catholic unity that brings lasting and true freedom to nations.

Kuyper says, "Thus notice I was not too bold when I claimed for Calvinism the honor of being neither an ecclesiastical, nor a theological, not a sectarian conception, but one of the principal phases in the general development of our human race" (34). In Kuyper's vision, Calvinism is a life system working to bring true freedom to every nation around the globe. Kuyper points to this reality in America. He says, "In America, where Calvinism has come to unfold itself in a still higher liberty, this commingling of blood is assuming a larger proportion than has ever yet been known" (37). By blood, Kuyper means all the different people groups that have come to America: Irish, German, English, Jewish, Spanish, African, etc. Even if these groups have not directly joined the Calvinist life system, they have still reaped the blessings of Calvinism because it was Calvinism that offered freedom to all of these groups via the American political structure established on Calvinistic principles. Kuyper places on the shoulders of Calvinism, rooted in the gospel, the ability to draw diverse peoples together offering true freedom to all.

One of the reasons Calvinism draws diverse people together is because it begins with the smallest and lowest parts of society. Kuyper says, "Thus far every forward movement had gone forth from the authorities in State, Church or Science, and from thence had descended to the people. In Calvinism, on the other hand, the peoples themselves stand out in their broad ranks and form a spontaneity of their own, press forward to a higher form of social life and conditions" (38). Calvinism rightly teaches that each man must live in the presence of God, and this means that every Calvinistic reformation occurs at the lowest level of the cosmos: individual responsibility before God. Individuals who have been changed by God's sovereign love are the ones who bring about true and lasting reformation in the world. This is the engine that runs the vision of the Calvinistic life system.

Kuyper concludes his first lecture by reminding his audience

> that only by Calvinism the psalm of liberty found its way from the troubled conscience to the lips; that Calvinism has captured and guaranteed to us our constitutional civil rights; and that simultaneously with this there went out from Western Europe that mighty movement which promoted the revival of science and art; opened new avenues to commerce and trade, beautified domestic and social life, exalted the middle classes to positions of honor, caused philanthropy to abound, and more than all this, elevated, purified, and ennobled moral life by puritanic seriousness. (40)

Calvinism and Religion

In his second lecture, Kuyper argues that Calvinism has a religious energy that other theological camps do not. This energy is found in how Calvinism places God and God's glory at the center of all religious life. This energy restores the true nature of religion, and this restoration in turn sets out the full task of man before God.

What is this religious energy in Calvinism? It is that all of the Christian religion must be for God. Kuyper says, "The starting-point of every motive in religion is God and not Man" (46). God should be our primary and ultimate goal. We must love and worship God for his own sake, not because we are trying to get a reward out of him. Kuyper upholds the high calling of Christianity: "to covet no other existence than for the sake of God, to long for nothing but for the will of God, and to be wholly absorbed in the glory of the name of the Lord, such is the pith and kernel of all true religion" (46). The true demand of the Christian life is that we must spend all our energy following God's will.

Placing God at the center of the Christian life undermines many of the religious errors in man. Kuyper says, "Religion *for the sake of man* carries with it the position that man has to act as a mediator for his fellow-man. Religion *for the sake of God* inexorably excludes everyhuman mediatorship" (48). Kuyper then makes a side comment about Augustine of Hippo, offering one brief critique of this early Christian. While Augustine was theologically accurate on many things, Kuyper points out that Augustine remained "the Bishop." Kuyper says that this title is problematic because it seems to imply that Augustine was an intermediary between his fellow man and God. Kuyper says that title and position is problematic because Augustine could not really stand between his fellow man and God. Only Jesus has that position.

Kuyper argues, "If, on the contrary, the demand of religion is that *every* human heart must give glory to God, no man can appear before God on behalf of another. Then every single human being must appear personally, for himself, and religion achieves its aim only in the *general priesthood of believers*" (48). In recognizing all Christians as priests before God, Kuyper and Calvin recover the true spirit of Christian liberty. Kuyper says it this way: "Only where all priestly intervention disappears, where God's sovereign election from all eternity binds the inward soul directly to God Himself, and where the ray of divine light enters straightway into the depth of our heart—only there does religion, in its most absolute sense, gain its ideal realization" (49).

Kuyper then pushes this religious fervor to the edges of life. He says, "God is present in all life, with the influence of His omnipresent and almighty power, and no sphere of human life is conceivable in which religion does not maintain its demands that God shall be praised, that God's ordinances shall be observed, and that every *labora* shall be permeated with its *ora* in fervent and ceaseless prayer" (53). When man is focused on God as the goal of all religion, this sweeps up all of man's life into a life of worship. In Calvinism, all of man's work becomes an act of doxology to God.

Kuyper summarizes this point: "Wherever man may stand, whatever he may do, to whatever he may apply his hand, in agriculture, in commerce, and in industry, or his mind, in the world of art, and science, he is, in whatever it may be, constantly standing before the face of his God, he is employed in the service of his God, he has strictly to obey his God, and above all, he has to aim at the glory of his God" (53).

THE TRUE CHURCH

Kuyper then takes this vision—the Christian religion being focused on God—and he applies this to the church herself.

Kuyper looks at the nature of salvation. He says that salvation as a work of God will be a complete and total work. This is not universalism (where everyone will be saved) but it is a universal work. Kuyper says it this way: "To be sure, many branches and leaves fell off the tree of the human race, yet the tree itself shall be saved; on its new root in Christ, it shall once more blossom gloriously. For regeneration does not save a few isolated individuals, finally to be joined together mechanically as an aggregate heap. Regeneration saves the organism, itself, of our race" (59). Ultimately, our salvation is not about us but about God and his glory, which means that God will bring about the salvation of his creation. All creation must worship him alone, and so God's glory necessitates a work of salvation that reaches all creation.

Given that religion is for God, he will not allow anyone or anything to get in the way of right worship of him. Kuyper condemns errors in other denominations, particularly Roman Catholicism (what he calls Romanism) which try to put something between God and his people: building structures, confessionals, priests, etc. When Christians are called by God, he calls them directly to himself. So while in this life, we are on a pilgrimage, this is not a trip that starts way off in a distant country. Rather, Kuyper describes our pilgrimage as one that starts at the door of the house of God and continues walking into the sanctuary of God (61).

This excludes the idea of an institutional church dispensing grace out to the weary traveler on his way to salvation. There is no partial salvation for believers. Salvation is a one-time event that places the person directly before God. God does not need extra help from an institution to save us. Kuyper says this means there is no salvation after death because a Christian is already saved in Jesus. This also excludes saying masses for the dead or teaching that people can be saved after death. The church does not help in the process of salvation. Salvation is a full and pure work of God.

Kuyper then turns to explain what the church is. He says, "For Calvin, the Church is found in the *confessing individuals themselves,*—not in each individual separately, but in all of them taken together, and united, not as they themselves see fit, but according to the ordinances of Christ" (62). The church is found in the people who make up the body of Christ, not an institution or hierarchy.

Kuyper says, "But if the Church consists in the *congregation of believers*, if the churches are formed by the union of confessors, and are united only in the way of confederation, then the differences of climate and of nation, of historical past, and of disposition of mind come in to exercise a widely variegating influence, and multiformity in ecclesiastical matters must be the result" (63–64).

Here Kuyper gives a robust defense for all the diverse ways that Christians have worshiped God over the years and centuries. Different congregations will worship with different music and different liturgies and different languages because the church is made up of different people and different people groups. To try to claim that all churches must have the same liturgy or the same music or the same language is wrong. God has planted his people in different times and cultures and places, and their churches will look different because of that. This is not a problem. This is a glorious feature of the gospel spreading throughout the world.

Kuyper correctly says, "The Church of Christ is not national but ecumenical. Not one single state, but the whole world is its domain" (65). This means that every tribe, tongue, people, and land must worship God, and its worship will include every language and music and liturgy imaginable because each congregation will worship with the gifts and talents that it has in its culture.

CALVINISM AND THE PRACTICAL LIFE

Kuyper then argues that this vision of right religion changes everything in our practical lives. He says that a Christian "is a pilgrim, not in the sense that he is marching through a world with which he has no concern, but in the sense that at every step of the long way he must remember his responsibility to that God so full of majesty, who awaits him at his journey's end" (69–70). The fact that we owe God everything in our lives changes everything in our lives.

It is not just that we need to be invested in this life, but that we must also recognize how God is invested in the world. Kuyper describes God's involvement in the world as the "ordinances of God." God has thought out the world and all its ways, and we see this all around us in the various works of creation.

Kuyper says, "So, there are ordinances of God for the firmament above, and ordinances for the earth below, by means of which this world is maintained, and, as the Psalmist says, These ordinances are the servants of God. Consequently, there are ordinances of God for our bodies, for the blood that courses through our arteries and veins, and for our lungs as the organs of respiration. And even so are there ordinances of God, in logic, to regulate our thoughts; ordinances of God for our imagination, in the domain of aesthetics; and so, also, strict ordinances of God for the whole of human life in the *domain of morals*" (70).

These ordinances of God reveal the foundation for all our actions as Christians in the world. We are to imitate God's care for the world in how we live in the world. We are not to separate ourselves from the world but to seek it out and embrace it.

Kuyper offers a wonderful critique of Anabaptism which is a significant problem in our own time. He says, "The avoidance of the world has never been the Calvinistic mark, but the shibboleth of the Anabaptist . . . . They refused to take the oath; they abhorred all military service; they condemned the holding of public offices. Here already, they shaped a new world, in the midst of this world of sin, which however has nothing to do with this our present existence" (72–73). This Anabaptist vision is a faulty one. It tries to claim that God is not concerned about the world around us, and so we should pull away and hide from it. Kuyper says the Anabapist tries to create two worlds: one for Christians and one for secularists. But Kuyper rejects that idea. God is personally invested in the world and he has established ordinances for all of life. This means Christians cannot be faithful to God unless they move into the world in an effort to bring all the world into subjection to him: music, art, farming, politics, philosophy, education, business, etc.

Kuyper says this about the Christian: "He feels, rather, his high calling to push the development of this world to an even higher stage, and to do this in constant accordance with God's ordinance, for the sake of God, upholding, in the midst of so much painful corruption, everything that is honorable, lovely, and of good report among men" (73). The world was made by God and for God. This means the Christian must point everyone and everything to that God. It is all for him.

Kuyper closes out this lecture saying, "Calvinism understood that the world was not to be saved by ethical philosophizing, but only by the restoration of tenderness of conscience. Therefore it did not indulge in reasoning, but appealed directly to the soul, and placed it face to face with the Living God, so that the heart trembled at His holy majesty, and in that majesty, discovered the glory of his love" (76–77).

Calvinism and Politics

In his third lecture, Kuyper shows how Calvinism has impacted politics over the last several centuries. Calvinism has had this impact because it has placed special focus on God's sovereignty. This teaching impacts all areas of authority in the world: state, society, and church. Every authority in the world must submit to the highest authority: the sovereign God. Kuyper accurately holds up God's sovereignty over the state.

THE NATURE OF THE STATE

Kuyper first begins by explaining the nature of the state, its origin and position in the world. He says,

"For, indeed, without sin there would have been neither magistrate nor state-order; but political life, in its entirety, would have evolved itself, after a patriarchal fashion, from the life of the family" (80). He also describes the state as a crutch for a lame leg. In a perfect world, this crutch would not be needed, but in a fallen world, the state is a gift of God set up and established under his authority.

Kuyper then draws out two key lessons. First, that we should gratefully receive the state from the hand of God and second, that we should recognize "that, by virtue of our natural impulse, we must ever watch against the danger which lurks, for our personal liberty, in the power of the state" (81). Kuyper saw correctly that the state is a necessary authority, but it also must be restrained.

Kuyper points out two ways it should be restrained. First, he says, "No man has the right to rule over another man, otherwise such a right necessarily, and immediately becomes the *right of the strongest*" (82). Every authority is an authority by God's grace. People might elect the person, or the person might inherit an office of authority, but there is nothing inherent in that particular person which gives him authority over other people. Which is to say, all authority is derived from God's authority. This leads to Kuyper's second means of restraint: God is the ultimate authority in all spheres. God's authority restrains the authority of the state.

Kuyper then explains, "God's own direct government is absolutely *monarchial*" (83). He adds, "But Calvin considered a co-operation of many persons under mutual control, i.e., *a republic*, desirable, now that a mechanical institution of government is necessitated by reason of sin" (83).

This is a key comment and deserves further reflection. While I agree with Kuyper that the universe is an absolute monarchy, I would point to C.S. Lewis who, following Richard Hooker's view, describes our universe as a constitutional monarchy.[2] The constitution of our universe is Scripture, especially the law of God which he gave his people at Sinai.

In saying this, I am not suggesting that this constitution is *over* God as a human constitution would be over a human king. Instead, we must understand that the law originates in God. This means that the law of God is not arbitrary rules, but that God's nature and the expression of his nature that we have in his Word are fixed and consistent. This does not mean that God is controlled by something outside of himself but rather that his nature is unchanging and eternal.

2. Michael Ward, *Planet Narnia* (Oxford, Oxford University Press, 2008), 67.

In this way, we see that God's law is a constitution for our benefit. The law of God reveals God's nature to us. This is not to suggest that we can use that law against God and remove him from his position. That would be impossible. That would be like using God against God. His nature does not contradict itself. The important point then is to realize that this cosmic constitution is God's gracious love to us; he gives it to us so that we can know how to live under his monarchy.

This brief discussion is important because it shows how a constitution, like the US Constitution, is an important feature of a government system. A constitution is not just a necessity brought about by sin but it is actually a design supported by God's word.

THE AMERICAN STATE

Kuyper turns to reflect on the American state and gives a robust defense for understanding the American republic as one based on God's law. Kuyper cites several key quotes from our foundational documents.

He quotes from the Declaration of Independence which speaks "of the law of nature and of nature's God" and "the Supreme Judge of the world for the rectitude of our intentions." As well as the Articles of Confederation, which says, "It hath pleased the great Governor of the world to incline the hearts of the legislators." Several of the state constitutions written in that same period say that they are "grateful to Almighty God for the civil, political and religious liberty, which He has so long permitted us to enjoy and looking to Him, for a blessing upon our endeavors" (86). Given these statements, we see that the American republic was established as a state under the authority of the sovereign God. Kuyper understood this reality, while many Christians today sadly doubt it or are ignorant of it.

Kuyper also explains how the American War for Independence was different from the French Revolution in 1789. The French Revolution sought to establish a state based on atheism. Kuyper says, "It is a sovereignty of the people therefore, which is perfectly identical with atheism" (88). To build a state solely on the people's opinions is to do so with an atheistic foundation which functionally ignores God and God's law.

Kuyper then critiques the Germanic philosophy of the state which claims that the state is the highest good. This political philosophy elevates the state to become "a mystical conception" (88). This idea suggests that the state has perfect knowledge of what is best for its people. Kuyper explains, "There is no other right, but the immanent right which is written down in the law. The law is right, not because its contents are in harmony with the eternal principle of right, but because *it is law*. If on the morrow it fixes the very opposite, this also must be right" (89). This mysticism of the state continues to our own day, which is a key reason the state has sought to overreach its true position and take control of so much. The state believes itself to be a god.

Kuyper, however, reminds us that even if the state tries to claim divinity for itself, the reality is that there is always a higher authority over it. This points us to our true and everlasting hope: "And however powerfully the State may assert itself and oppress the free individual development, above that powerful State there is always glittering, before our soul's eye, as infinitely more powerful, the majesty of the King of kings, Whose righteous bar ever maintains the right of appeal for all the oppressed, and unto Whom the prayer of the people ever ascends, to bless our nation and, in that nation, us and our house!" (90).

WHAT IS THE STATE FOR?

Kuyper then turns to the true role of the state. He says that the state bears the sword through three means: first, justice, which includes corporeal punishment; second, war, to defend against enemies; third, order, to thwart forcible rebellion inside the country.

Kuyper then reminds his audience that God's sovereignty means all authorities must obey God, so every citizen is called to pursue true liberty. He says, "And thus the struggle for liberty is not only declared permissible, but is made a duty for each individual in his own sphere . . . . by causing all men, the magistrates included, to bow in deepest humility before the majesty of God Almighty" (98–99).

Magistrates of the state are called to establish true liberty. Kuyper says, "They have to serve God, by ruling the people according to *His* ordinances" (103). He says they do this in these key ways: acknowledging that God is the supreme ruler, encouraging all to honor the Sabbath, proclaiming days of prayer and thanksgiving, and invoking his divine blessing.

Here Kuyper is arguing for a state that supports and encourages Christianity. But Kuyper does not want the state to supersede the church's authority. He says that "both church and state must, each in their own sphere, obey God and serve His honor. And to that end in either sphere *God's Word* must rule, but in the sphere of the state only through the conscience of the persons invested with authority" (104). The magistrate in the state must obey God's Word by submitting to it according to his conscience. This is not to make the state subservient to the church but to make the state subservient to God.

THE STATE AND RELIGION

Kuyper then turns to the important question, must the state decide which church denomination is the true one?

Kuyper answers with a strong no. But he is careful not to fall into prevalent errors here. He says that he gives this answer, "Not from a false idea of neutrality, nor as if Calvinism could ever be indifferent to what is true and what false, *but because the government lacks the data of judgment*, and because every magisterial judgment here *infringes the sovereignty of the Church*" (105).

Kuyper explains that the state has a sword, but it is not the spiritual sword. The state should keep out of the sphere of the church. The church has its own sphere which the state must respect. The church should deal with errors in theology and sin with the spiritual sword that it has. The state must allow the church to deal with this issue. Kuyper explains further: "The Church may not be forced to tolerate as a member one whom she feels obliged to expel from her circle; but on the other hand no citizen of the State must be compelled to remain in a church which his conscience forces him to leave" (108). The civil magistrate should promote the Christian religion, but he may not force people to attend a certain church. The civil magistrate should also respect the ruling of a church pertaining to an issue of church membership and excommunication. Kuyper says, "Meantime what the government in this respect demands of the churches, it must practice itself, by allowing to each and every citizen liberty of conscience, as the primordial and inalienable right of all men" (108).

Kuyper concludes this lecture saying, "A nation, consisting of citizens whose consciences are bruised, is itself broken in its national strength" (108). This summarizes the key problem in America today: we are a nation of bruised consciences. Given our troubled souls and minds, it is no wonder that we have lost the strength to pursue true liberty under God and so we rely on a broken state to fix us. Meanwhile our souls lie in the torments of sin.

Calvinism and Science

In his fourth lecture, Kuyper argues that Calvinism has had a positive impact on the field of science. He says it has done this in four key ways: fostering a love for science, restoring its proper domain, setting it free from unnatural bonds, and solving what Kuyper calls the "unavoidable *scientific conflict*" (110).

CALVINISM FOSTERED A LOVE OF SCIENCE

First, Kuyper shows how Calvinism encourages a true love of science. The love of science is bound up with a love of God's character, specifically his sovereign will in everything. Kuyper says it this way: "But if you now proceed to the decree of God, what else does God's fore-ordination mean than the certainty that the existence and course of all things, i.e., of the entire cosmos, instead of being a plaything of caprice and chance, obeys law and order, and that there exists a firm will which carries out its designs both in nature and in history?" (114). The very ground of scientific investigation rests upon the way God has orchestrated and ordained the world. In a random world, there would be no laws of nature for science to study. It is only in a world governed by the fatherly eye of God that there can be real science.

Kuyper says, "Thus you recognize that the cosmos, instead of being a heap of stones, loosely thrown together, on the contrary presents to our mind a monumental building erected in a severely consistent style" (114). We do not live in an evolving pond of goo but in a grand cathedral with stained glass windows and ornate flying buttresses. All of it is designed by the hand of a loving artist.

Kuyper concludes this point: "Faith in such an *unity*, *stability*, and *order* of things, personally, as predestination, cosmically, as the counsel of God's decree, could not but awaken as with a loud voice, and vigorously foster love for science" (115).

CALVINISM RESTORED SCIENCE'S DOMAIN

Kuyper then turns to how science fared in other times and eras. In the late medieval age, science languished and was chained down by the Roman Catholic church, a terrible despot. Kuyper says, "Christendom, it must be confessed, did not escape this error. A dualistic conception of regeneration was the cause of the rupture between the life of nature and the life of grace. It has, on account of its too intense contemplation of celestial things, neglected to give due attention to the world of God's creation" (118). The erroneous divide between nature and grace in the late medieval age sorely abused science and discouraged true scientific exploration.

Kuyper reminds us that the creeds of the church, by contrast, confess that God is "Maker of heaven and earth," and in light of that, we must also explore the earth in order to understand our maker. He points out that "the final outcome of the future . . . is not merely spiritual existence of saved souls, but *the restoration of the entire cosmos*" (119). Given the cosmic scope of salvation, we mustinvestigate all of the cosmos in order to bring it under the lordship of Christ. Kuyper says this is what the Calvinistic confessions did in speaking "of two means whereby we know God, *viz.*, the Scriptures *and Nature*" (120).

In the medieval age, the church taught a hierarchy of being which meant that spiritual things were superior to earthly things, making the earthly less important. Kuyper illustrates this idea by pointing to the clergy, who ranked higher than the laity, and then the monks, who were higher than the clergy. This structure pushed nature away and did not encourage a robust study of nature as a way to know and love God. Kuyper says, "Everything uncountenanced and uncared for by the church is looked upon as being of a lower character, and exorcism in baptism tells us that these lower things are really meant to be unholy" (123). The natural world was banished to the realm of the unholy and so could not reveal God. As such, it was not as important as so-called spiritual matters. But Kuyper pushes back that idea, saying, "not only *the church*, but also *the world* belongs to God and in both has to be investigated the masterpiece of the supreme Architect and Artificer" (125).

Kuyper summarizes this point, saying, "A Calvinist who seeks God, does not for a moment think of limiting himself to theology and contemplation, leaving the other sciences, as of a lower character, in the hands of the unbelievers; but on the contrary, looking upon it as his task to know God in *all* his works, he is conscious of having been called to fathom with all the energy of his intellect, things *terrestrial* as well as things *celestial*" (125).

CALVINISM SET SCIENCE FREE

Kuyper next traces the rise of the university and how it was subjugated to the authority of the pope and the Vatican. Kuyper says "Rome did oppose, not only *in* the Church, what was right, but also beyond its boundaries, the freedom of the word" (128). The church suppressed free inquiry in the scientific realm. Kuyper says that in this era, "The right of free inquiry was unknown" (128). He then points to the example of Descartes, who, having "had to leave Roman Catholic France, found among the Calvinists of the Netherlands . . .a safe retreat" (129). Descartes, a philosopher who was Roman Catholic, was not free in France, but he found freedom in a Calvinistic country. He still found rivals to his philosophy there, but there was freedom of thought and true scientific inquiry. Something a Roman Catholic country could not endure.

Kuyper forcefully remarks, "As long, however, as the Church stretched out her *velum* over the entire drama of public life, the state of bondage naturally continued, because the only object of life was to merit heaven . . ." (129). The church in the late medieval age overreached its sphere of authority and tried to forbid science from growing and flourishing. It was the Reformation and particularly Calvinism that set science free. Kuyper explains: "This blessedness, for every true Calvinist, grows out of regeneration, and is sealed by the perseverance of the saints. Where in this manner the 'certainty of faith' supplanted the traffic of indulgences, Calvinism called Christendom back to the order of creation: 'Replenish the earth, subdue it and have dominion over everything that lives upon it'" (130). When a Christian rightly understands the secure gift of salvation, he is freed to pursue a a joyful exploration and study of nature which is rightly understood as a gift from our heavenly Father who has redeemed us from sin and delights in us studying his creation. Only the free gift of salvation can set science free.

Kuyper summarizes: "The cosmos, in all the wealth of the kingdom of nature, was spread out before, under, and above man. This entire limitless field had to be worked. To this labor the Calvinist consecrated himself with enthusiasm and energy" (130).

CALVINISM SOLVES THE CONFLICT IN SCIENCE

Finally, Kuyper turns to the conflict in science between unbelieving systems of worldliness and the true Christian worldview, e.g., naturalism versus supernaturalism. We see this conflict in our own day, and it was one that Kuyper saw in his day as well. Kuyper says, "Free investigation leads to collisions" (130). This is one result of truly free scientific investigation. However, this collision is not between faith and science as some might suggest. The reality is, there is no conflict between these two. Kuyper correctly says, "Every science in a certain degree starts *from faith*" (131). The true conflict then is between naturalists and supernaturalists. Or, as Kuyper labels the two sides, normalists and abnormalists.

The normalists "reject the very idea of creation, and can only accept evolution" (132). While the abnormalists: "adhere to primordial creation over against an *evolutio in infinitum*" (132). The normalists are the ones who believe in purely natural forces in the world, so they try to cling to the evolutionary process since it seems to be an explanation based on purely natural forces, while the abnormalists recognize that there are both natural and supernatural forces in the world, so they accept influences beyond the physical realm. But the key is to recognize as Kuyper does that "*each [has] its own faith*" (133).

This continues to be the primary conflict in science today. Kuyper rightly recognizes that both are "in earnest, disputing with one another *the whole domain of life*" (133). It is not like evolution is merely about origins. It is a life system and so it is diametrically opposed to everything in the Christian life system. Kuyper explains that the opposing system of the normalists arose in the eighteenth century and took up "a position at the center" of the scientific community (135). And from that position, this materialistic perspective has impacted all areas.

But Kuyper shows how this materialist position is not consistent with the nature of the world. He primarily focuses on how the normalist position cannot account for human consciousness. He says that Calvinism "goes back to *human consciousness*, from which every man of science has to proceed as *his* consciousness" (136). Science has no way to explain this phenomenon, so the normalist just assumes it on faith while at the same time denying that it is supernatural or derived from a deity. Kuyper says, "Calvin, however, does not excuse unbelievers on this account. The day will come when they will be convinced in their own conscience" (137). There is no way of escape from this truth. Everyone will acknowledge the supernatural perspective because everyone is assuming it already and using it in their own minds.

So how do we win in this conflict?

Kuyper points back to Calvinism setting science free to pursue true investigation. This is the need of the hour, and the current lack of freedom has produced a languishing in the scientific community. He says, "*Free science* is the stronghold we defend against the attack of her tyrannical twin-sister" (138). This twin sister is the normalist position. It looks and acts like true science, but it is not really interested in true and free investigation. Instead, it is trying to suppress the supernatural position in the scientific community. Kuyper says, "The Normalist tries to do us violence even in our own consciousness. He tells us that our self-consciousness must needs be uniform with his own, and that everything else we imagine we find in ours stands condemned as self-delusion" (138). In Kuyper's time and in our own time, we see this relentless attack on the Christian perspective, and we know that we will be slighted and oppressed on this front, but we must not yield to the tyrants who are trying to control the sanctuary of our hearts.

Instead, Christian scientists must be bold. We must steal the tactics and courage from the opposing naturalists and pursue true scientific investigation. Kuyper says, "If the courage, the perseverance, the energy, which enabled [the normalists] to win their suit at last, will be found now in a still higher degree, with Christian scholars. May God grant it!" (139). Christian scholars must stand up and defend the truth and defend true scientific freedom.

Kuyper concludes by saying that if the church and state withdraw "in order that the university may be allowed to take root and flourish in its own soil, then certainly the division, which is already begun, will be accomplished of itself and undisturbed, and in this domain also it will be seen that only a peaceful separation of the adherents of antithetic principles warrants progress,—honest progress,— and mutual understanding" (140). Kuyper predicts that eventually the current government-controlled university system that is controlling science will collapse. He rightly sees that "the days of its artificial unity are numbered, that it will split up" (141). When that happens, then science will flourish in true freedom again.

Calvinism and Art

Kuyper begins his fifth lecture by acknowledging the terrible idol that art has become. He says, "Genuflection before an almost fanatical worship of art, such as our time fosters, should little harmonize with the high seriousness of life, for which Calvinism has pleaded, and which it has sealed, not with the pencil or the chisel in the *studio*, but with its best blood at the stake and in the field of battle" (142). Kuyper reminds his audience to see the vast difference between the artists in the art shop and the faithful life that Christian men and women are called to live in following Christ. While art does make an impact on culture and society, it does not inspire the saints to die for it.

Kuyper adds, "Moreover the love of art which is so broadly on the increase in our times should not blind our eyes, but ought to be soberly and critically examined" (142). We should not create art for the sake of art, nor should we enjoy it for itself. We must produce art for God's sake and glory. This means a high and serious examination of all art in order to bring it in submission to God.

Kuyper recognizes the way art so often becomes a separate religion. Those who reject true religion and spirituality will seek for religious experiences anywhere they can find it. He says, "And, unable to grasp the holier benefits of religion, the mysticism of the heart reacts in an art-intoxication" (143). One of the common ways people create a false religion is by succumbing to the worship of art. But Kuyper says the way to avoid that error is to keep our "eyes fixed upon the Beautiful and the Sublime in its eternal significance, and upon art as one of the richest gifts of God to mankind" (143). If we see art as a good gift from God, then we can keep art in its proper place and use it as a tool for God's service.

Kuyper turns to three key topics in art: religion and art, art in the worldview of Calvinism, and how Calvinism promotes art.

CALVINISM HAD NO RELIGIOUS ART

Kuyper points out that Calvinism did not develop an art style of its own, as other schools or religions have done.

Kuyper explains why Calvinism did not develop its own art style. He begins by looking to the new covenant and how God has given his people a more glorious mode of worship than what can be found in the old covenant. He says, "But when this ministry of shadows has served the purposes of the Lord, Christ comes to prophesy the hour when God shall no longer be worshipped in the monumental temple at Jerusalem, but shall rather be worshiped in spirit and in truth. And in keeping with this prophecy you find no trace or shadow of art for worship in all the apostolic literature" (147). Aaron's visible priesthood gives way to the invisible priesthood after the order of Melchizedek. Kuyper describes it this way: "The purely spiritual breaks through the nebula of the symbolical" (147).

Kuyper argues that the older forms of religion were symbolic and ornamental because that was the more immature way to worship. He says, "Originally Divine worship appeared inseparably united to art, because, at the lower stage, Religion is still inclined to lose itself in the aesthetic form" (148). He then points out how God matures his people: "The more, on the other hand, Religion develops into spiritual maturity, the more it will extricate itself from art's bandages, because art always remains incapable of expressing the very essence of Religion" (148).

Kuyper then uses an analogy to show how religion and art start out looking very similar to each other, but when they are more mature, we can see how very different they really are. He says this is like two babies who look the same when they are in the cradle but when they reach adult maturity, you can tell that one is a man and the other is a woman. He says, "And so, arrived at their highest development, both Religion and Art demand an independent existence, and the two stems which at first were intertwined and seemed to belong to the same plant, now appear to spring from a root of their own" (148).

Kuyper concludes this point saying, "Calvinism was neither able, nor even permitted, to develop an art-style of its own from its religious principle. To have done this would have been to slide back to a lower level of religious life" (149).

ART IN CALVINISM

Kuyper then turns to consider how art fits in the worldview of Calvinism. He reminds his audience that religion must stay in its place: "However holy

Religion may be, it must keep within its own bounds, lest, in crossing its lines, it degenerate into superstition, insanity, or fanaticism" (152). He then quotes John Calvin who says, "All the arts come from God and are to be respected as Divine inventions" (153). As a direct gift from God, art must be free to pursue its high calling before God. Art must be in service to God but that does not necessarily mean art should be controlled by the church.

Rather, Kuyper shows how art is not just for the church or for Christians but actually a good gift to all men. He says, "In all Liberal Arts, in the most as well as in the least important, the praise and glory of God are to be enhanced. The arts, says [Calvin], have been given us for our comfort, in this our depressed estate of life" (153).

Being a gift for all people does not lessen the high calling of art. Kuyper says, "In view of all this we may say that Calvin esteemed art, in all its ramifications, as a gift of God, or, more especially, as a gift of the Holy Ghost" (153). This gift of the Holy Ghost is a general grace to all men, but it is also a constant reminder that all artists must submit to God.

Kuyper then argues that art is designed to show us the good and the beautiful that this world has lost through the corruption of sin and death. He says, "But if you confess that the world once *was* beautiful, but by the curse has become *undone*, and by a final catastrophe is to pass to its full state of glory, excelling even the beautiful of paradise, then art has the mystical task of reminding us in its productions of the beautiful that was lost and of anticipating its perfect coming luster" (155). Art, when it reaches its full glory, points to the original form of the world and suggests the coming renewal of all creation at the hand of the supreme artist.

In this way, we see that art is not intended to be a means of subjective expression but must instead point to objective reality. God sets boundaries that art must obey. Kuyper says, "If God is and remains Sovereign, then art can work no enchantment except in keeping with the ordinances which God ordained for the beautiful, when He, as the Supreme Artist, called this world into existence" (155). The power of art is something that God created, and art has power only in so far as God has granted it that power. Kuyper adds, "And all this because the beautiful is not the production of our own fantasy, nor of our subjective perception, but has an objective existence, being itself the expression of a Divine perfection" (156).

Kuyper pushes this further saying that since all creation is for God, ultimately all art and all beauty are for God. He says, "Imagine that every human eye were closed and every human ear stopped up, even then the beautiful remains, and God sees it and hears it." (156). Even the parts of this world that humans cannot see—distant galaxies, deep-sea creatures—all of these are wonderful works of art that God by himself enjoys.

Kuyper summarizes this point saying that every artist has to seek out his art and practice his skill. This does not mean that the artist should look into himself, but rather he must look to an objective standard outside himself in order to grow in his craft. And this reinforces the key idea that art is something that comes from outside the artist; art is something that is found in God himself (156).

CALVINISM PROMOTES ART

Kuyper argues that Calvinism encourages and promotes art. He says this happens because Calvinism sees art as a gift of common grace to all men. He says, "Calvinism, on the contrary, has taught us that all liberal arts are gifts which God imparts promiscuously to believers and to unbelievers, yea, that, as history shows, these gifts have flourished even in a larger measure outside the holy circle" (160).

Kuyper then paints a wonderful picture for Christians: "The world after the fall is no lost planet, only destined now to afford the Church a place in which to continue her combats; and humanity is no aimless mass of people which only serves the purpose of giving birth to the elect. On the contrary, the world now, as well as in the beginning, is the theater for the mighty works of God, and humanity remains a creation of his hand, which, apart from salvation, completes under this present dispensation, here on earth, a mighty process, and in its historical development is to glorify the name of Almighty God" (162).

Art also plays an important role because "art reveals ordinances of creation which neither science, nor politics, nor religious life, nor even revelation can bring to light" (163).

Kuyper summarizes this point saying that Calvin sends the three powers—science, religion, and art—out to permeate all human life: "There must be a *Science* which will not rest until it has thought out the entire cosmos; a *Religion* which cannot sit until she has permeated every sphere of human life; and so also there must be an *Art* which, despising no single department of life adopts, into her splendid world, the whole of human life, religion included" (163).

So what art has Calvinism promoted in the world?

Kuyper suggests his own Dutch poets as one key example. In the English-speaking world, we can also see this influence in many famous poets: Edmund Spenser,

John Milton, William Shakespeare, and many others. In painting, Kuyper points to Rembrandt van Rijn's fine works. In music, Claude Goudimel produced many great psalms and hymns for Christians.

Kuyper also traces out several key ideas that have impacted art. First, the gospel highlights the dignity of all men. He says, "If a common man, to whom the world pays no special attention, is valued and even chosen by God as one of His elect, this must lead the artist also to find a motive for his artistic studies in what is common and of every-day occurrence, to pay attention to the emotions and the issues of the human heart in it, to grasp with his artistic instinct their ideal impulse, and, lastly, by his pencil to interpret for the world at large the precious discovery he has made" (166).

Kuyper also points out how sorrow and suffering in the world points to and highlights the suffering of Jesus in his ministry and work on the cross. He says, "And if thus far the eyes of all had been fixed constantly and solely upon the sufferings of the 'Man of Sorrows,' some now began to understand that there was a mystical suffering also in the general woe of man, revealing hitherto unmeasured depths of the human heart, and thereby enabling us to fathom much better the still deeper depths of the mysterious agonies of Golgotha" (166–167).

Kuyper concludes this lecture by addressing those who complain about the lack of Calvinistic art today. He says they should be careful how they complain. Kuyper asks, "Has that man any right to complain about the stillness of the forest, who with his own hand has caught and killed the nightingale?" (170).

Calvinism and the Future

In his sixth and final lecture, Kuyper begins by summarizing his past lectures with these words: "[Calvinisim] raised our Christian religion to its highest spiritual splendor; it created a church order, which became the preformation of state confederation; it proved to be the guardian angel of science; it emancipated art; it propagated a political scheme, which gave birth to constitutional government, both in Europe and America; it fostered agriculture and industry, commerce and navigation; it put a thorough Christian stamp upon home-life and family-ties; it promoted through its high moral standard purity in our social circles; and to this manifold effect it placed beneath Church and State, beneath society and home-circle, a fundamental philosophic conception strictly derived from its dominating principle, and therefore all its own" (171).

Kuyper then moves on to look at his current time and to suggest where Calvinism can help in shaping and building for the future. He states the topic of his final lecture as *"A new Calvinistic development needed by the wants of the future"* (171).

THE CURRENT SITUATION

Kuyper recognizes the many technological changes in his era. He says, "World-intercourse and communication are constantly becoming more rapid and widespread. Asia and Africa, until recently dormant, gradually feel themselves drawn into the larger circle of stirring life" (172).

Kuyper then describes the current ailment in Western culture. He rightly saw in his own time that there was a spiritual darkness rising in the world that threatened both the present and the future. The solution he proposes is that we recover a robust understanding of the spiritual solution that our world is seeking. He says, "Our personal life as men and citizens subsist not in the comforts that surround us, nor in the body, which serves us as a link with the outward world, but in the spirit that internally actuates us" (172). He then points to Nietzsche as a prime example of where men are: "Nietzsche may give us offence by his sacrilegious mockery, still what else is his demand for the '*Ubermensch*' (over-man), but the cry of despair wrung from the heart of humanity by the bitter consciousness that it is spiritually pining away?" (173). Kuyper suggests that his time is very much like the Golden Age of Rome—both are "rotten to the very core" (173).

The light then that we need is not to be found in other sources. He says, "But this light did not arise through evolution; it shone from the Cross of Calvary" (174). Rejuvenation can come only through the old and yet ever new gospel. Modern philosophy tries to suggest that it has outgrown Christianity. Kuyper acknowledges that "the responsibility of this degeneration undoubtedly rests in part with the Christian churches themselves, not excepting those of the Reformation" (175).

HISTORY OF THE PROBLEM

Kuyper then turns to describe how society had arrived at this dark time. He looks again at the French Revolution of 1789 as the source of many of the philosophical and moral problems. He says, "Man as such, each individual henceforth, was to be his own lord and master, guided by his own free will and good pleasure" (176). He continues, "From France this spirit of dissolution, this passion of wild emancipation, has spread among the other nations, especially through the medium of an infamously obscene literature, and infected their lives" (177).

Kuyper then says, "The spirit of this *modern life* is most clearly marked by the fact that it seeks the origin of man not in creation after the image of God, but in evolution from the animal" (p 178). Looking to evolution to explain all of life leads to two errors. First, evolution lowers man from bearing the image of God to being nothing more than a material organism. Second, evolution denies the sovereignty of God, leaving everything in the hands of blind process.

With these evolutionary factors at work, the outcome is that "money, pleasure, and social power, these alone are the objects of pursuit; and people are constantly growing less fastidious regarding the means employed to secure them. Thus the voice of conscience becomes less and less audible." (179).

Kuyper comments that this endless and restless process wearies the human soul. He says, "Deprived of the wholesome influence of rest, the brain is over-stimulated and over-exerted till the asylums are no longer adequate for housing the insane" (179).

The emphasis on evolution means that everything and anything can be changed. One example is the institution of marriage. Kuyper says, "The cause of monogamy is no longer worth fighting for, since polygamy and polyandry are being systematically glorified in all products of the realistic school of art and literature" (179).

With the influence of evolution, "Gradually the conflict between the strong and the weak has grown to be the controlling feature of life, arising from Darwinism itself, whose central idea of a *struggle for life* has for its mainspring this very antithesis" (179).

IS ROME AN OPTION?

Kuyper then turns to consider one possible solution to this wide-spread problem. He considers whether the church of Rome can offer a solution to this dilemma.

Kuyper says, "Though the history of the Reformation has established a fundamental antithesis between Rome and ourselves, it would nevertheless be narrow-minded and shortsighted to underestimate the real power which even now is manifest in Rome's warfare against Atheism and Pantheism" (183). He sees that the church of Rome is holding its position well against the work of these enemy forces. However, Kuyper does acknowledge many points that cannot be reconciled between Protestants and Roman

Catholics: ecclesiastical hierarchy, man's nature, justification, the Mass, invocation of saints, worship of images, purgatory, and others. He says that we are as "unflinchingly opposed to Rome as our fathers were" (183).

Kuyper then suggests how the Roman church can be a helpful cobelligerent in the fight. He says that the lines of the battle are drawn this way: theism versus pantheism, sin versus perfection, divine Jesus versus mere man, atonement versus example to imitate. In these kinds of fights, Rome can be a helpful cobelligerent to the Calvinistic position (183). However, does this mean that our future should be sought in the work of Rome?

Kuyper offers a resounding no. He looks to South and Central America for what Rome can offer. He says, "But in vain do we look in those American Romish States for a life which elevates, develops energy, and exerts a wholesome influence outside" (184). He also looks at Europe and says, "In Europe, also, the credit of all the Protestant states is high, that of the southern countries which are Roman Catholic, is at a painful discount" (185).

In this way, we can see that Rome does not have the answers that our society needs. In fact, Kuyper suggests going to Rome for help "would be a step backwards in the course of history" (186).

Instead, Kuyper says that Protestantism is the truly forward-looking work.

Kuyper acknowledges that some will scoff at this claim. He says that these ones will say, "Ye yourselves have no right to make a stand on Protestantism; for after Protestantism came Modernism" (187). However, he objects to this by saying that modernism was not a forward movement at all, so it was not really the production of Protestantism. He says, "What Modernism offers us is not modern, but rather very antique; not posterior, but anterior to Protestantism, reaching back to the Stoa and to Epicurus" (187).

CALVINISM MUST BE RESTORED

Kuyper urges a return to Calvinism as the only true advancement, because it truly proclaims the great work of inward renewal that must happen in every individual in order to reform society. Kuyper says, "[Jesus] healed the sick body, but He even more truly bound up our spiritual wounds" (188). Other philosophies merely work to restore the bodily ailments with little to no look at the internal and spiritual needs of the man. In this way, Kuyper says, "Only of Calvinism can it be said that it has consistently and logically followed out the lines of the Reformation" (190).

Kuyper lays out four key ways for us to recover Calvinism. First, Calvinism should be supported more. Second, Calvinism must be a central subject of study. Third, Christians must apply Calvinism to our time. Fourth, churches that confess Calvinism must not be ashamed of their confession.

Kuyper reminds his American audience of the great Christian and Calvinistic roots in our country. He says, "And when your President proclaims a national day of thanksgiving, or when the houses of Congress assembled in Washington are opened with prayer, it is ever new evidence that through American democracy there runs even yet a vein which, having sprung from the Pilgrim Fathers, still exerts its power at the present day" (192–193).

From these and other fruits around us, we must see the true heritage we have in Calvinism. Kuypers says, "What I demand then, and demand with an historic right, is that this ungrateful ignoring of Calvinism shall come to an end" (193). Christian churches around the world and in America need to stop being ashamed of their Calvinistic confession (194).

ELECTION NOT SELECTION

Kuyper concludes this final lecture by elaborating on the great threat of his day and ours: evolution. He says, "Our generation turns a deaf ear to *Election*, but grows madly enthusiastic over *Selection*" (195). These are the two sides in the fight: election versus natural selection. Is a holy and just God the sovereign Judge over the world or is a naturalistic process of selection blindly grinding away?

Kuyper insightfully says that natural selection "attempts to solve this problem of problems" (196). He continues: "Even in the single cell it posits differences, weaker and stronger elements. The stronger overcomes the weaker, and the gain is stored up in a higher potency of being" (196). In this way, selection is trying to be the answer to every question in the universe. In making this claim, we see that there is no neutral ground to be found. Selection takes all or nothing.

Kuyper also reminds his audience that "Calvinism dared to face this same all-dominating problem, solving it, however, not in the sense of a blind selection stirring in unconscious cells, but honoring the sovereign choice of Him Who created all things visible and invisible" (197). Calvinism is a life system as well, and it submits to the sovereign election of God. Kuyper says, "The quickening of life comes not from men: it is the prerogative of God" (199).

Kuyper declares that the battle lines have been drawn between materialism and Christianity. There is no reconciling the two sides of election and selection. Everything hangs upon these two starkly opposite foundations.

Calvinism is a cry to rally the troops under the banner of God's sovereign election. It is only there, at the foot of God's divine plan, that salvation can be found. And this salvation in Christ orients everything else out in the world. Calvinism is the need of the hour. But it is not Calvinism that saves. It is Jesus that saves.

Kuyper closes his lecture series, reminding his audience that it is the election of God that brings about true revival. Nothing that man does can make a difference unless God is at work.

Kuyper says it this way: "Now, let Calvinism be nothing but such an Aeolian Harp,—absolutely powerless, as it is, without the quickening Spirit of God—still we feel it our God-given duty to keep our harp, its strings tuned aright, ready in the window of God's Holy Zion, awaiting the breath of the Spirit" (199).

May our Calvinistic harps be always ready, and may the Spirit come quickly and make our lives resound again.

Additional Resources for Further Study

Abraham Kuyper, *Wisdom and Wonder: Common Grace in Science and Art*, Ed. Jordan J. Ballor, Trans. Nelson D. Kloosterman, 2011.

W. Robert Godfrey, *John Calvin: Pilgrim and Pastor*, Crossway: Weaton, Illinois, 2009.

David N. Steel and Curtis C. Thomas, *The Five Points of Calvinism: Defined, Defended and Documented*, Presbyterian & Reformed Publishing Co., 1963.

Kuyper's Public Theology set, Lexham Press, lexhampress.com.

Kuyperian Commentary for both resources on Abrahm Kuyper and other cultural and political writings that continue Kuyper's vision, kuyperian.com.

Printed in Great Britain
by Amazon